TONY COOKE

Because the
LORD *is my*
SHEPHERD

THE TWELVE BLESSINGS OF AN EMPOWERED LIFE

Published by Harrison House Publishers Shippensburg, PA 17257

ISBN Tradepaper: 978-1-68031-672-8

ISBN eBook: 978-1-68031-673-5

Connect with us on

f Facebook @ HarrisonHousePublishers

and 🅞 Instagram @ HarrisonHousePublishing

so you can stay up to date with news

about our books and our authors.

Visit us at **www.harrisonhouse.com**

for a complete product listing as well as

monthly specials for wholesale distribution.

The Harrison House Vision

Proclaiming the truth and the power

of the Gospel of Jesus Christ with excellence.

Challenging Christians

to live victoriously,

grow spiritually,

know God intimately.

CONTENTS

Introduction

As I write these words, our country has just passed the one-month mark of the "shut down" in response to the coronavirus pandemic that has brought paralysis and chaos into the world. Myriads of people have experienced massive disruptions in their lives, and for some, this truly has been a journey through the valley of the shadow of death. Fear has been gnawing at the souls of millions of people, and uncertainty abounds. Threats of many kinds seem to surround us.

But in the midst of all of this, a great beacon of light shines with laser-like precision and intensity. This illumination inspires a hope that will not be denied, and it can be summed up in five simple words: *"The Lord is my shepherd."* For believers, this cherished phrase releases a stream of comforting sentiments and beautiful images—ones that proceed from the 23rd Psalm.

The LORD is my shepherd; I shall not want. He makes me to lie down in green pastures; He leads me beside the still waters. He restores my soul; He leads me in the paths of righteousness for His name's sake. Yea, though I walk through the valley of the shadow of death, I will fear no evil; for You are with me; Your rod and Your staff, they comfort me. You prepare a table before me in the presence of my enemies; You anoint my head with oil; my cup runs over. Surely goodness and mercy shall follow me all the days of my life; and I will dwell in the house of the LORD forever.

What makes this the most beloved of all psalms for multitudes of the faithful, and what makes it one of the most recognized sections of the Bible throughout the world? That is what this small book is about.

In these pages we will discover why we are never alone, never without help, and never without hope. As we journey with David through this timeless pastoral poem, we will explore the significance and meaning of the words that flowed out of David's heart as he reflects on God's goodness. The good news is that God does not show favoritism, and the Lord who was David's Shepherd is ours as well.

As you study and meditate upon this psalm, remember that it is actually a song David wrote. Can you picture him spending nights on the hills around Bethlehem, sitting under the expanse of the Milky Way, keeping an eye on the flock as he played his lyre (a type of harp) and worshipped God with songs (psalms) he had composed? David was a man after God's own heart (1 Samuel 13:14, Acts 13:22), and he was called *"the sweet psalmist of Israel"* (2 Samuel 23:1). His insights resonate powerfully with our hearts today.

WHAT DOES IT MEAN TO HAVE A SHEPHERD?

David knew exactly what he was talking about when he penned the 23rd Psalm. He was an experienced shepherd who cared deeply for his father's flock. He was tremendously conscientious and relentlessly committed to the sheep under his watch, and he knew that the Lord was even more committed to him. Even as a youth, David stated:

"I have been taking care of my father's sheep and goats," he said. *"When a lion or a bear comes to steal a lamb from the flock, I go after it with a club and rescue the lamb from its mouth"* (1 Samuel 17:34-35, NLT).

This correlates perfectly with what Jesus taught. After identifying Himself as the Good Shepherd, Jesus explains:

The good shepherd sacrifices his life for the sheep. A hired hand will run when he sees a wolf coming. He will abandon the sheep because they don't belong to him and he isn't their shepherd. And so the wolf attacks them and scatters the flock. The hired hand runs away because he's working only for the money and doesn't really care about the sheep (John 10:11-13, NLT).

David was no hireling and neither is Jesus. He is faithful and entirely trustworthy, and He won't abandon you when trouble comes.

The more you come to know the Lord as your Shepherd, the more you are persuaded that He is completely committed to you and your well-being. Just like David's father entrusted the care of his sheep to David, God entrusted the care of His sheep to Jesus, and He is a good and faithful Shepherd.

> *I give them eternal life, and they will never perish. No one can snatch them away from me, for my Father has given them to me, and he is more powerful than anyone else. No one can snatch them from the Father's hand* (John 10:28-29, NLT).

The commitment that Jesus expresses toward us is not merely theoretical or conceptual; it is so concrete that He backed it up by sacrificing Himself for us. God's power was demonstrated when He raised Jesus from the dead to secure our forgiveness and bring us into an everlasting covenant with Himself. We receive these wonderful benefits by faith—by placing our trust in who He is and what He did for us.

ISAIAH REVEALS THE SHEPHERD

When God wanted to convey His compassion and tenderness toward us, He used the imagery of a shepherd.

> *He will feed His flock like a shepherd; He will gather the lambs with His arm, And carry them in His*

bosom, And gently lead those who are with young (Isaiah 40:11).

That is so remarkable! When we did wrong, God came to our rescue. He redeemed us when we had fallen into sin. The greatest expression of love occurred when Jesus bore our sins and shed His blood for us on the cross! Paul states, *"God demonstrates His own love toward us, in that while we were still sinners, Christ died for us"* (Romans 5:8). When we were at our very worst, God gave us His very best.

Jesus, our Great Shepherd, further communicates and amplifies the magnitude of God's amazing love.

What do you think? If a man has a hundred sheep, and one of them goes astray, does he not leave the ninety-nine and go to the mountains to seek the one that is straying? And if he should find it, assuredly, I say to you, he rejoices more over that sheep than over the ninety-nine that did not go astray. Even so it is not the will of your Father who is in heaven that one of these little ones should perish (Matthew 18:12-14).

I once heard someone suggest that it doesn't make a lot of sense for a shepherd to leave the ninety-nine to pursue the one unless you happen to be that one. That is the beauty of God's love for us. As Augustine said, "God loves each of us as if there were only one of us."

Before we look at the benefits of following the Shepherd (which are many), it is important to recognize the fallacy of desiring Jesus to be our Savior without necessarily wanting to follow Him as our

Shepherd. If I assert that *"the Lord is my Shepherd,"* but I don't truly aspire to follow Him, I am only fooling myself. This doesn't mean that any of us have followed Him perfectly, but it does imply that we should be completely dedicated to cooperating with His oversight, guidance, and direction in every area of our lives. His Word and His Spirit should govern us. I am not speaking here of serving Him in our own strength but yielding to His empowering grace.

None of us have followed God flawlessly in the past, and this is where God's mercy comes in. This is why repentance and recommitment are important. In spite of past missteps, we can have a gloriously radiant future. All of us can likely identify with Peter's statement: *"Once you were like sheep who wandered away. But now you have turned to your Shepherd, the Guardian of your souls"* (1

Peter 2:25, NLT). The old hymn—"Come Thou Fount of Every Blessing"—articulates it perfectly:

> Jesus sought me when a stranger
>
> Wandering from the fold of God
>
> He, to rescue me from danger
>
> Interposed His precious blood

It is because of the blood of Christ that we have forgiveness, relationship, and covenant with God. Our Shepherd truly gave His life for us so we could become partakers of eternal life and enter into an everlasting covenant with the Heavenly Father. The author of Hebrews expresses this so powerfully!

Now may the God of peace—who brought up from the dead our Lord Jesus, the great Shepherd of the sheep, and ratified an eternal covenant with his blood—may he equip you with all you need for doing his will. May he produce in you, through the power of Jesus Christ, every good thing that is pleasing to him. All glory to him forever and ever! Amen (Hebrews 13:20-21, NLT).

PARTAKING OF HIS BENEFITS

The 23rd Psalm is David's confession of faith; it is a declaration of who God was in his life, as well as a description of God's role in providing and caring for him. Instead of us simply admiring David's relationship with his Shepherd, this is intended to be exemplary. In other words, the Lord will care for and guide us, just as He did David. As we observe David relating to God in the varied dimensions of His goodness, we can also cultivate our faith in these aspects of God's compassion and concern for us.

So what are the benefits of having the Lord as our Shepherd? David articulates them plainly and clearly. There are six verses in Psalm 23, and in the following pages I will identify twelve specific blessings that are released into our lives as we follow the Great Shepherd.

Blessing One: PROVISION

"I shall not want."

(Psalm 23:1)

"I shall not want" carries the idea of not lacking anything, and God has clearly and consistently articulated His desire to be our Provider! David recognizes this elsewhere when he writes, *"I have been young, and now am old; yet I have not seen the righteous forsaken, nor his descendants begging bread"* (Psalm 37:25).

As Israel was concluding their journey through the wilderness, Moses said, *"The LORD your God has blessed you in everything you have done. He has watched your every step through this great wilderness. During these forty years, the LORD your God has been with you, and you have lacked nothing"* (Deuteronomy 2:7, NLT). If God could provide for them for forty years in the desert, he can certainly take care of us. Likewise, the psalmist declares,

> *For the LORD God is a sun and shield; the LORD will give grace and glory; no good thing will He withhold from those who walk uprightly* (Psalm 84:11).

After talking about how people often worry about material needs such as clothing and food, Jesus admonishes us to *"… seek first the kingdom of God and His righteousness, and all these things shall be added to you"* (Matthew 6:33). It has often been said that Jesus does not mind us having things; He simply doesn't want things having us.

As Paul writes to his friends in Philippi, he remembers with gratitude their generosity toward him and calls their gift *"a sweet-smelling aroma, an acceptable sacrifice, well pleasing to God."* He then joyfully states, *"And my God shall supply all your need according to His riches in glory by Christ Jesus"* (Philippians 4:18-19). What a comfort to know that we have a God who loves, cares, and provides for us.

There is another dimension of *"I shall not want"* that goes beyond merely having necessary material things, and this brings us to the concept of contentment. I remember hearing of a little girl who was trying to quote the 23rd Psalm. She inadvertently said, "The Lord is my Shepherd, that's all I want." Her slight miscue actually turns out to be very insightful. When our heart is fixed and we are trusting in the Lord, there is an amazing sense of contentment that fills our souls. We are not grasping to obtain fulfillment through material things that bring no true satisfaction. We are not envying what others have, telling ourselves that we will never truly be happy until we have _____ (fill in the blank).

Being content with what we have does not necessarily come naturally; Paul describes it as a skill he had to learn. He states, *"I have learned how to be content (satisfied to the point where I am not disturbed or disquieted) in whatever state I am"* (Philippians 4:11, AMPC). It seems that much of "not wanting" is found in the secret of being content.

A big part of contentment is based on being so in love with Jesus Himself that earthly things pale by comparison. You can enjoy things (see 1 Timothy 6:17) without being obsessed with things. Do you recall the words of the old hymn?

> Turn your eyes upon Jesus
>
> Look full in His wonderful face
>
> And the things of earth will grow strangely dim
>
> In the light of His glory and grace

Nikolaus Zinzendorf was a great church leader in the eighteenth century who was so enamored with Jesus that He became the focus of his affection and attention. Zinzendorf said, "I have but one passion; it is the love of Him, nothing but Him!" It is good to know that God is committed to providing us with that which is necessary, but it is also good to remember that material things do not represent the ultimate issues of life.

Don't be obsessed with money but live content with what you have, for you always have God's presence. For hasn't he promised you, "I will never leave you alone, never! And I will not loosen my grip on your life!" (Hebrews 13:5, TPT).

Perhaps we can look at it this way: God has promised to meet all of our needs, and He has also promised to *be* the fulfillment of our ultimate need—our need of Him.

Blessing Two: REST

"He makes me to lie down in green pastures."

(Psalm 23:2)

We live in a society that is full of tired people. Busyness is often a badge of honor worn by people to express their value. Many people live at breakneck speed, never slowing down to really enjoy life, never taking time to "smell the roses." Jesus worked, but He also took time to rest. In one instance we read, *"Then Jesus said, 'Let's go off by ourselves to a quiet place and rest awhile.' He said this because there were so many people coming and going that Jesus and his apostles didn't even have time to eat"* (Mark 6:31, NLT).

Part of God's original plan for us is that we be able to rest. God Himself rested on the seventh day after He had completed His magnificent work of creation. I don't think God rested because He was tired and worn out, but in part, to set a necessary example for us. Work and rest are both part of God's plan for man, and while we are not under the "Law of the Sabbath" any longer, there is certainly a principle of Sabbath that remains.

One of Jesus' most beloved statements pertains to the offer of rest that He extends:

> *Come to Me, all you who labor and are heavy laden, and I will give you rest. Take My yoke upon you and learn from Me, for I am gentle and lowly in heart, and you will find rest for your souls. For My yoke is easy*

and My burden is light (Matthew 11:28-30).

There are powerful verses elsewhere in Scripture about God's desire for us to rest.

- *Rest in the LORD, and wait patiently for Him* (Psalm 37:7).

- *Those who live in the shelter of the Most High will find rest in the shadow of the Almighty* (Psalm 91:1, NLT).

- *For thus says the Lord GOD, the Holy One of Israel: "In returning and rest you shall be saved; In quietness and confidence shall be your strength"* (Isaiah 30:15).

Charles Spurgeon once noted, "Rest time is not waste time. It is economy to gather fresh strength," and he is absolutely right. God does not want to exhaust us; He wants to refresh us. That is why, when we allow Him to be our Shepherd, He makes us to lie down in green pastures.

It is good to note here that "rest" involves more than just the physical. Our bodies need rest, but so do our minds. Some of our minds need a break, especially if we are the kind of person whose mind is always dealing with problems. Some people are constantly analyzing, speculating, theorizing, and trying to solve every problem—even problems that haven't happened yet. God is the One who gave us our brains, and He expects us to use them. However, He does not want us "trusting" our brains instead of Him. Your brain is a good tool, but it is a bad god.

If you have trouble lying down in green pastures, consider these two passages of Scripture:

LORD, my heart is not proud; my eyes are not haughty. I don't concern myself with matters too great or too awesome for me to grasp. Instead, I have calmed and quieted myself, like a weaned child who no longer cries for its mother's milk. Yes, like a weaned child is my soul within me (Psalm 131:1-2, NLT).

Trust in the LORD with all your heart, and lean not on your own understanding (Proverbs 3:5).

The Good Shepherd will give us rest for both our body and our mind. It is good to work and be productive, but we honor God and fulfill part of His plan for our lives when we *"rest in the Lord"* (Psalm 37:7), trusting confidently in Him.

Blessing Three: PEACE

"He leads me beside the still waters."
(Psalm 23:2)

The term *still* waters paints a most attractive picture of serenity, tranquility, and peace. In a world with so much agitation and turmoil, we should always be mindful of that sense of calm and security that only comes from *"the Prince of Peace"* (Isaiah 9:6). Famed author C. S. Lewis wisely states, "God cannot give us a happiness and peace apart from Himself, because it is not there. There is no such thing."

To lead us into peace, Jesus points us directly to Himself. He states, *"Let not your heart be troubled; you believe in God, believe also in Me…Peace I leave with you, My peace I give to you; not as the world gives do I give to you. Let not your heart be troubled, neither let it be afraid*" (John 14:1, 27). The prophet Isaiah asserts, *"Perfect, absolute peace surrounds those whose imaginations are consumed with you; they confidently trust in you"* (Isaiah 26:3, TPT).

Peace abides in our lives when we know and trust in the faithfulness of God, when we rest in the One who committed to never leaving us and never forsaking us (Hebrews 13:5). Michelangelo, the Italian painter and sculptor, wisely said, "Do not fret, for God did not create us to abandon us."

Anxious thoughts will present themselves, but the still waters are available and our Shepherd will skillfully lead us into that place of peace. Paul gives us some great instructions on experiencing God's peace. He writes:

> *Don't worry about anything; instead, pray about everything. Tell God what you need, and thank him for all he has done. Then you will experience God's peace, which exceeds anything we can understand. His peace will guard your hearts and minds as you live in Christ Jesus... Fix your thoughts on what is true, and honorable, and right, and pure, and lovely, and admirable. Think about things that are excellent and worthy of praise. Keep putting into practice all you learned and received from me—everything you heard from me and saw me doing. Then the God of peace will be with you* (Philippians 4:6-9, NLT).

Even though David wrote these beautiful words about the still waters, he was not exempt from the worries and cares that are so common to the human experience. He learned, though, by following His Shepherd how to arrive at the place of still waters. Consider how David, at different times, cooperated with God and moved from episodes of anxiety into peace.

- *David was greatly distressed....but David encouraged and strengthened himself in the Lord his God* (1 Samuel 30:6, AMPC).

- *In the multitude of my anxieties within me, Your comforts delight my soul* (Psalm 94:19).

- *I said to myself, "Relax and rest. GOD has showered you with blessings"* (Psalm 116:7, MSG).

Through difficult seasons, David had mastered the art of talking to himself and reminding himself of God's faithfulness. Even in times of emotional upheaval, David had learned to commit himself to God's goodness. It was there—trusting in God's goodness—where David found the still waters, and it is there that we will find them also. Remember the words of the Puritan preacher Thomas Watson: "If God be our God, He will give us peace in trouble. When there is a storm without, He will make peace within. The world can create trouble in peace, but God can create peace in trouble."

Blessing Four:

RESTORATION

"He restores my soul."

(Psalm 23:3)

There are people who love to restore old cars. They will buy an older classic or maybe a muscle car and then restore it. To restore something means to bring it back to its former condition. For example, we might say that a person who had become sick was restored to health. Jeremiah writes, *"For I will restore health to you and heal you of your wounds,' says the LORD"* (Jeremiah 30:17).

The world we live in can be a rough place. People have been hurt, disappointed, neglected, abused, ignored, insulted, and injured in countless ways. Life bruises and afflicts, but Jesus heals and restores. Think about the woman caught in adultery (see John 8:2-11). Everyone was judgmental and condemning toward her. No one cared about her life, much less her emotional well-being. It was Jesus who demonstrated mercy, grace, and compassion. Through the compassion of God, He restored her dignity and sense of value.

Jesus also shared a story about a traveler who was robbed, beaten severely by thieves, and abandoned (see Luke 10:30-37). Even though he was "half dead" and religious people had passed him by, a Samaritan man had compassion on him, administered first aid, and took him to a place where he could be cared for and could recuperate. It was that merciful, restorative approach that Jesus commended, and He encouraged us to *"Go and do likewise"* (Luke 10:37).

It is God's nature to restore, and He wants us to demonstrate that heart of restoration toward others. Paul writes, *"Brethren, if a man is overtaken in any trespass, you who are spiritual restore such a one in a spirit of gentleness, considering yourself lest you also be tempted"* (Galatians 6:1).

David prayed for restoration after he had sinned, and he tells us that the Lord restores our soul. Elsewhere David prays, *"Restore to me the joy of Your salvation, and uphold me by Your generous Spirit"* (Psalm 51:12). The prophet Isaiah also describes the marvelous restoring nature of the Lord:

> *The high and lofty one who lives in eternity, the Holy One, says this:*

43

"I live in the high and holy place with those whose spirits are contrite and humble. I restore the crushed spirit of the humble and revive the courage of those with repentant hearts" (Isaiah 57:15, NLT).

What is it that has been taken from you that you need restored? What about your peace, your joy, your sense of well-being? He is the Great Shepherd who restores your soul!

Blessing Five: GUIDANCE

*"He leads me in paths of righteousness
for His name's sake."*

(Psalm 23:3)

There are three aspects of this phrase: (1) He leads me, (2) in paths of righteousness, and (3) for His name's sake. Each of these is important. Our Shepherd cares about us, and He leads us in the right way, in godly paths. Not only do we benefit when we follow His guidance, but it always results in His glory and in His name being honored.

God has given us numerous assurances that He is committed to giving us guidance and direction in our lives. For example,

Psalm 32:8 states, *"I will instruct you and teach you in the way you should go; I will guide you with My eye."* Scripture also tells us, *"the Lord directs the steps of the godly"* (Psalm 37:23, NLT), and we are admonished, *"In all your ways acknowledge Him, and He shall direct your paths"* (Proverbs 3:6).

The question is not so much whether God desires to give us guidance in life, but rather, do we really want His guidance? He did not promise to lead us in paths of convenience or of fleshly gratification but in paths of righteousness. Being led in His paths involves a willingness to be obedient on our part. Consecration is a factor as well, and we must answer the question, "Is our heart totally surrendered to do His will?"

Two factors in faithfully and accurately following God are our relationship with His Word and His Spirit. God has given us an entire Bible so we can know His mind, His will, and His ways. Scripture is full of His wisdom and His counsel. This is why the psalmist affirms, *"Your word is a lamp to my feet and a light to my path"* (Psalm 119:105). Through God's Word, our paths are made clear, and because they are illuminated, we do not stumble.

The Holy Spirit also will guide us. Because He inspired the writing of Scripture, He will never guide us contrary to the written Word of God. Rather, He will help us make wise applications of what He already has said in the Bible. The Holy Spirit is a Person—the third member of the Trinity—and because He is a Person, we should not be surprised that He would guide us. Paul attests to this in Romans 8:14 when he states, *"For as many as are led by the Spirit of God, these are sons of God."* As we allow God to lead us into paths of righteousness for His name's sake, we will see a fulfillment in our lives of what the psalmist declared, *"You guide me with your counsel, leading me to a glorious destiny"* (Psalm 73:24, NLT).

Blessing Six: SECURITY

"Though I walk through the valley of the shadow of death, I will fear no evil; for You are with me."

(Psalm 23:4)

The 23rd Psalm is loved for so many reasons, but it is perhaps the fourth verse that causes it to be such a source of comfort during the most traumatic and difficult times of life. In spite of the harsh challenges life throws at us, we hear and are comforted by these words, *"I will fear no evil; for You are with me."* In the words of an old hymn, when we are leaning on His everlasting arms, we truly are "safe and secure from all alarms."

While this psalm vividly portrays God's comfort and support, it does not ignore the hard realities of human existence. Rather, David's words show us the power and care of a Shepherd whose influence penetrates and transcends even the worst that life can throw at us. Being a follower of Jesus does not make us exempt from the challenges of life. In Psalm 34:19, David writes, *"Many are the afflictions of the righteous, but the LORD delivers him out of them all."*

It is important to note the words, *"Though I walk through…"* David does not talk about setting up camp or settling down in the valley of the shadow of death, but rather, walking through it. The life of faith is a journey, and we embrace the reality of what Paul teaches when he states, *"For our light affliction, which is but for a moment, is work-ing for us a far more exceeding and eternal weight of glory"* (2 Corinthians 4:17).

David and Paul are not denying the reality of the problems but are simply recognizing them as temporal. We acknowledge the reality of life's difficulties, but we believe that God's love and power are greater. While David recognizes he might walk *through* the valley of the shadow of death, he also writes a few verses later, *"And I will dwell in the house of the LORD forever"* (Psalm 23:6). The valley is temporary, but the presence and glory of God are eternal.

Another vital part of David's faith is his declaration that he will fear no evil because he knows that God is with him. Some people read such a statement and feel intimidated because they find themselves struggling with fear. But it is important to remember that having strong faith is the result of a growing process, and people should not feel condemned if their faith is not perfect. One man was honest with Jesus, saying, *"Lord, I believe; help my unbelief"* (Mark 9:24), and Jesus helped him. The Lord did not condemn or reject him.

We even see levels of growth in David's faith in Psalm 56. In verse three, David states, *"Whenever I am afraid, I will trust in You."* David acknowledges here that when he is afraid, he will put his trust in God. But in verse four he writes, *"In God I have put my trust; I will not fear."* Some might look at this and mistakenly conclude that David is contradicting himself in these two statements, but he is not. Have you ever struggled at a given time, only to step up to a higher level of trust or to a greater degree of faith later? That is what David did here.

If you feel like your faith is weak, don't focus on yourself or your faith. Rather, set your attention on God and His Word. The more you focus on yourself, the more you will struggle. The more you focus on God and His Word, the stronger your faith will grow. But regardless of whether you feel your faith is weak or strong, remember that you have a great God, and His love for you is not based on the perfection of your faith.

The faith that grows in your heart—the kind of trust that comes from the truth of God's Word—engenders great benefits and blessings. After admonishing the reader to *"Trust in the Lord with all of your heart"* (Proverbs 3:5), Solomon proceeds to describe one of the benefits of walking in God's ways: *"When you lie down, you will not be afraid; yes, you will lie down and your sleep will be sweet"* (Proverbs 3:24).

The results of trusting and relying on God are described powerfully in another psalm as well: *"They do not fear bad news;*

they confidently trust the LORD to care for them. They are confident and fearless and can face their foes triumphantly" (Psalm 112:7-8, NLT). Because David knew his Shepherd and God's heart and faithfulness, he was confident no matter what kind of challenges he went through in life, God would be with him. Because of that, he need not fear any evil.

Blessing Seven: COMFORT

"Your rod and Your staff, they comfort me."

(Psalm 23:4)

When David mentions being comforted by his Shepherd's rod and staff, it is a continuation of what he had said about not fearing any evil, even as he went through the valley of the shadow of death. The rod and staff are vital tools for a shepherd, and they aid him greatly in protecting and caring for the sheep. The rod was typically a formidable club the shepherd used to kill predators. Jesus speaks of the tenacity of the shepherd when a wolf came to attack the flock—the shepherd will never abandon the sheep (John 10:12-13).

Shepherds were not defenseless, and David understood this very well. David's weapon of choice in his most famous battle—the one with Goliath—was the sling, and it proved to be very lethal. But David was also very familiar with the power of the rod. Consider what he said to King Saul as he described his background experiences:

> *"I have been taking care of my father's sheep and goats," he said. "When a lion or a bear comes to steal a lamb from the flock, I go after it with a club and rescue the lamb from its mouth. If the animal turns on me, I catch it by the jaw and club it to death. I have done this to both lions and bears…"* (1 Samuel 17:34-36, NLT).

David knew that his sheep were safe when he had his rod—his club. No wonder David was comforted thinking about the rod of his Shepherd, a rod that represents the power and authority of God Almighty!

It has been observed that Psalm 22, 23, and 24 provide prophetic glimpses of Jesus in His various roles: past, present, and future. From our perspective today, Psalm 22 portrays Jesus in His past role as the One who suffered on the cross. Psalm 23 presents Jesus in His present role as our Shepherd. Psalm 24 depicts Jesus in His future role as King of Kings and Lord of Lords.

When you put all these together, you have a more comprehensive picture of who Jesus is in His entirety. If we can borrow a thought from Psalm 24 and consider it in the light of the rod in Psalm 23, it is most impressive. In addition to His role as the

Shepherd, Jesus is also *"The LORD, strong and mighty; the LORD, invincible in battle"* (Psalm 24:8, NLT). No wonder David was comforted when he thought about his Shepherd being with him through the valley.

David also was consoled when he thought about the staff his Shepherd carried. A staff was also a stick but typically different than the rod. While the rod was more of a club for fending off predators, the staff was usually a longer stick used for walking (keeping balance), and it sometimes had a hooked end that was good for reaching around the body of a sheep that had fallen to help it back up. The staff was also good for helping to guide the sheep. If a sheep needed a gentle tap to keep from putting itself in danger or heading in the wrong direction, that staff was an extension of the shepherd's caring hands.

When I think of the "extension" aspect of the shepherd's staff, it reminds me that we are never outside of God's reach. Isaiah proclaimed, *"Behold, the LORD'S hand is not shortened, that it cannot save"* (Isaiah 59:1). In Psalm 139, David may have been thinking along the same lines when he talked extensively about the fact that no matter where he went, God would be with him. It was in this context that he joyfully states, *"I can never escape from your Spirit! I can never get away from your presence!"* (Psalm 139:7, NLT).

David paints a picture in Psalm 23 of a faithful Shepherd who was with him even as he walked through his darkest days. In spite of the difficulties during that phase of his life, David's faith rose above his fears, and he drew great comfort from the power and presence of God. It is almost as though David was walking in the light of what Jesus, the Great Shepherd, would say centuries later: *"I give them eternal life, and they will never perish. No one can snatch them away from me, for my Father has given them to me, and he is more powerful than anyone else. No one can snatch them from the Father's hand"* (John 10:28-29, NLT). This is why David did not fear; this is why David was comforted.

Blessing Eight:

SUSTENANCE

"You prepare a table before me in the presence of my enemies."

(Psalm 23:5)

David described a tremendously challenging season in the previous verse, and yet he sensed the support and strength of his Shepherd. In order to make any journey, especially a difficult one, an individual needs sustenance. Do you remember when Elijah was making an arduous trip and an angel came to him and gave him fresh hot bread? The Bible states, *"the food gave him enough strength to travel forty days and forty nights"* (1 Kings 19:8, NLT).

I have no doubt that there was a supernatural element involved in Elijah's situation, but it is important to remember that God wants to sustain and nourish us! Jesus said, *"I am the bread of life. He who comes to Me shall never hunger, and he who believes in Me shall never thirst"* (John 6:35), and Peter referred to *"the pure milk of the word"* (1 Peter 2:2). The Shepherd not only accompanied David on his trek, but also provided him with the nourishment he needed to make his pilgrimage successfully. We shall be sustained as well.

The New Living Translation renders this verse, *"You prepare a **feast** for me in the presence of my enemies"* (Psalm 23:5). That sounds like God, doesn't it? Perhaps we could look at this as a prophetic foreshadowing of the marriage supper of the Lamb (Revelation 19:9). However, at the table David describes, there is a huge difference—the meal described in Psalm 23:5 is served *"in the presence of my enemies."* That is a far cry from heaven; in the eternal state *"there shall be no more death, nor sorrow, nor crying. There shall be no more pain, for the former things have passed away"* (Revelation 21:4).

It is clear that Psalm 23 does not take place in heaven. We have no enemies in heaven, and there is no valley of the shadow of death there. And yet, God is with us in the here and now! In the midst of all life's challenges and disappointments, we have a Great Shepherd. It is one thing to think of God nourishing us and providing us with sustenance in the normal course of life, but this banquet is prepared for us in the presence of our enemies.

It is as though God is declaring to every opposing force, "I don't care how much you threaten My people—you will not prevail! I am undergirding them and sustaining them, and I will never leave them." Then I can imagine God turning toward us and boldly declaring, *"No weapon formed against you shall prosper"* (Isaiah 54:17). After that, I can imagine God telling us that we must eat and take nourishment for the journey as He spreads the table!

I remember reading this verse in times past thinking how counterintuitive it would seem to eat when in the presence of enemies. In my reasoning, this would not seem like a time to eat. Why? Enemies represent a threat. Threats can translate into fear and anxiety, and that kind of emotional agitation can produce a lack of appetite. People are different. Some have an increased appetite when they are stressed, but many people who are anxious experience a significant decrease in their hunger. Even in Scripture, Hannah refused to eat when she was in distress (1 Samuel 1:7), as did Saul when he was deeply troubled (1 Samuel 28:23).

After the Jews had rebuilt the walls of Jerusalem during the time of Nehemiah following the Babylonian captivity, the long-neglected Word of God was read to the people. Great conviction came upon the people, and they began to weep, presumably because they saw how short they had fallen from God's standards. Instead of encouraging their mourning, Nehemiah admonishes them:

> *Go and celebrate with a feast of rich foods and sweet drinks, and share*

gifts of food with people who have nothing prepared. This is a sacred day before our Lord. Don't be dejected and sad, for the joy of the LORD is your strength! (Nehemiah 8:10, NLT)

What an amazing statement! Feasting is not associated with weeping and mourning but with rejoicing and celebrating.

When passing through a valley or encountering "enemies" during your journey, you may have a reaction that does not feel or look anything like rejoicing. Don't get down on yourself. You are human, and you have emotions. The experience of some people may parallel what David describes in Psalm 30:5, *"Weeping may endure for a night, but joy comes in the morning."* Regardless of what you feel or experience, let me encourage you to look for the table that your

Shepherd has prepared for you. He wants to nourish you and sustain you in your journey. You can feast even in the presence of your enemies.

Blessing Nine: ANOINTING

"You anoint my head with oil."

(Psalm 23:5)

The act of anointing was readily understood in biblical times, more so than today. In the Mediterranean world, olive oil was common and was used in many aspects of daily life. It was used in cooking, in providing light (oil lamps), medicinally, and as a lotion and moisturizer. A gracious host would sometimes anoint a guest with fragrant perfume as an act of hospitality and respect. These are just a few of the practical functions of oil in biblical days.

A fascinating example of oil used in hospitality is seen when Jesus was dining with a Pharisee named Simon. Scripture tells us that an immoral woman from that community came to Jesus and brought *"a beautiful alabaster jar filled with expensive perfume"* (Luke 7:37, NLT). Other Pharisees were upset at her presence and her actions, but Jesus remarks:

> *"Look at this woman kneeling here. When I entered your home, you didn't offer me water to wash the dust from my feet, but she has washed them with her tears and wiped them with her hair. You didn't greet me with a kiss, but from the time I first came in, she has not stopped kissing my feet. You neglected the courtesy of olive oil to anoint my head, but*

she has anointed my feet with rare perfume" (Luke 7:44-46, NLT).

Olive oil also played a big role in the religious life of the Jewish people. It was used ceremonially in the installation of priests and kings, and the meaning of the word *Christ* is "anointed one." The word, *anoint* means to rub or to smear with oil, and in the religious sense, it is referred to in sanctification—in setting someone (or a thing or a place) apart for a special, divine purpose. James also instructed spiritual leaders in the church to anoint the sick with oil (representing the Holy Spirit) as they prayed the prayer of faith over them.

Shepherds commonly used oil in caring for their sheep, and this is what David was referring to when he said, *"You anoint my head with oil"* (Psalm 23:5). The Common English Bible states, *"You bathe my head in oil"* while the New Century Version reads, *"You pour oil of blessing on my head."* It is easy to imagine the scene of a flock of sheep being led by a shepherd in the intense heat of the Middle East. Biting insects could always be a problem to sheep, so the oil a shepherd would use was not just a soothing and refreshing way of moisturizing the skin, but also served as a deterrent against the bugs that would try to bite the sheep, especially around the ears and the nose. If a sheep had been bitten, the oil would serve as an ointment to soothe the wound and aid in the healing process.

It is understandable why Psalm 45:7 refers to *"the oil of gladness,"* and this verse was later applied to Jesus Himself (see Hebrews 1:9). Jesus was the Christ—anointed to be the Savior of the world. We are the sheep of His pasture, and He shares the anointing of the Holy Spirit with us (see Acts 2:33). We are anointed with grace, comfort, and peace. He soothes us and helps heal our wounds. He refreshes us and gives us strength for our journey.

Blessing Ten: ABUNDANCE

"My cup runs over."

(Psalm 23:5)

The final part of verse five is a picture of overflow and abundance—*"My cup runs over."* If we continue looking at this through the lens of hospitality conveyed in the earlier part of the verse, we see that our Shepherd is indeed the most gracious host imaginable. He has truly received us as His honored guests; we are accepted and celebrated in a most extravagant way.

In a book published in the early 1800s, *Oriental Customs*, a Captain Wilson wrote about an experience he had that was like that spoken of by the Psalmist: "I once had this ceremony performed on me in the house of a great and rich Indian, in the presence of a large company. The gentleman of the house poured upon my hands and arms a delightful odoriferous perfume, put a golden cup into my hands, and poured wine into it until it ran over. Assuring me at the same time that it was a great pleasure to him to receive me, and that I should find a rich supply of my needs in his house."[1]

Our Shepherd receives us lavishly and extravagantly! He *"gives to all liberally"* (James 1:5) and He is *"able to do exceedingly abundantly above all that we ask or think"* (Ephesians 3:20).

When a lost sheep is recovered, the Shepherd does not stoically receive it back into the fold, but *"he rejoices more over that sheep than over the ninety-nine that did not go astray"* (Matthew 18:13). Do you remember the response of the father when his wayward son returned? The father said to his servants:

> *"Quick! Bring the finest robe in the house and put it on him. Get a ring for his finger and sandals for his feet. And kill the calf we have been fattening. We must celebrate with a feast, for this son of mine was dead and has now returned to life. He was lost, but now he is found."* So the party began (Luke 15:22-24, NLT).

Can you picture God having such a celebratory attitude toward you? Our cups overflow because of God's overflowing, boundless love for us. Can you picture God being toward you the way He is described by an Old Testament prophet?

> *For the LORD your God is living among you. He is a mighty savior. He will take delight in you with gladness. With his love, he will calm all your fears. He will rejoice over you with joyful songs* (Zephaniah 3:17, NLT).

When we understand God's nature and His immeasurable love toward us, it is not hard to believe He would fill our cups to overflowing. You have heard, no doubt, the old comparison: "The pessimist says, 'My cup is half empty,' but the optimist says, 'My cup is half full.'" That's a pretty valid observation, but I like it even more that the believer can proclaim, "My cup is running over!"

There is another reason why God would want our cups to overflow. We already established one reason is because He loves us and wants to demonstrate His own benevolence. But we must not miss the other reason. God wants us to have an overflow so we have the wherewithal to bless others. When Paul was receiving a special offering from various churches to help struggling saints in Judea, he told the Corinthians, *"And God is able to make all grace abound toward you, that you, always having all sufficiency in all things, may have an abundance for every good work"* (2 Corinthians 9:8). Right before that, Paul had told them that their abundance would provide for the lack that others were experiencing (2 Corinthians 8:14). All of this reminds us of what we have probably heard many times: We are blessed to be a blessing! Our cups overflow.

NOTE:

1. Freeman, James M. and Harold J. Chadwick. *Manners and Customs of the Bible*. North Brunswick, NJ: Bridge-Logos Publishers, 1998.

Blessing Eleven:

CONFIDENCE

"Surely goodness and mercy shall follow me all the days of my life."
(Psalm 23:6)

There is something beautiful about the word *surely*, especially when you are going through difficult times. There is no hesitation or uncertainty in David's voice. He is fully persuaded of God's enduring commitment to him. What is he saying about God's goodness and mercy following him? He is declaring that definitely, certainly, absolutely, indisputably, undoubtedly, and unquestionably the blessings of God will always be his! David did not say maybe, perhaps, possibly, or even "I hope so."

Some might read this and think to themselves, *I wish I had the kind of confidence that David had—sometimes I struggle with uncertainty.* It is tempting to look at someone like David, especially when he had just penned such powerful and beautiful words, and assume that he had always been on the mountaintop—that he had always had perfect faith. We can safely say that David's certitude was not always what it was when he wrote the timeless words in Psalm 23. If we back up ten psalms, we see David in a much less confident frame of mind:

How long, O LORD? Will You forget me forever? How long will You hide Your face from me? How long shall I take counsel in my soul, having sorrow in my heart daily? How long will my enemy be exalted over me? Consider and hear me, O LORD my God; enlighten my eyes, lest I sleep the sleep of death (Psalm 13:1-3).

It is tremendous when our faith is soaring, but God loves us even when our faith is struggling.

It should not cause us to respect David less when we see that his faith was not always the pinnacle of perfection. As a matter of fact, most of us find biblical heroes more relatable when we see their humanity. Perhaps that is why James states, *"Elijah was as human as we are"* before he reminded them of how powerful Elijah's prayers had been (James 5:17, NLT). After David considers one more question in Psalm 13, he moves into what we might call the "victory side" of the equation. After his agonizing comments in the first four verses, he transitions to a declaration of faith:

> *But I have trusted in Your mercy; My heart shall rejoice in Your salvation. I will sing to the LORD, because He has dealt bountifully with me* (Psalm 13:5-6).

We should not allow ourselves to get condemned if we experience a time of frustration or questioning. We should keep our eyes on Jesus, our Great Shepherd, and continue to feed on His Word. As we look to Him, our faith will grow, and our trust will soar.

It is noteworthy that David envisioned two specific attributes of the Lord following him all the days of his life—God's goodness and mercy. Some variation of the phrase, *"The Lord is good and His mercy endures for-ever"* is found several times throughout the Old Testament and six times in various psalms. How important it is to be per-suaded that God is both good and merciful! These are intrinsic elements of God's very nature, and because of His commitment to us, we can be persuaded that goodness and mercy will follow us all the days of our lives.

Blessing Twelve: UNION

"I will dwell in the house of the LORD forever."

(Psalm 23:6)

As we reviewed earlier, the trials of life are transitory, and problems are temporary. Our relationship with God, though, is enduring and eternal. It is easy to read the last phrase of Psalm 23 and assume that David is merely saying, "When I die, I will go to heaven." While it is true that believers go to heaven when they leave this earth, that is not the real import of what David is saying. "Dwelling in the house of the Lord" does not begin when we die and go to heaven; it really starts when we enter into relationship with God.

As wonderful as heaven will be, we can dwell with Him now! Psalm 90:1 declares, *"Lord, You have been our dwelling place in all generations."* The very next psalm states, *"You have made the LORD your dwelling place"* (Psalm 91:9, ESV). It is true that we will dwell with the Lord forever (throughout eternity), but it is equally true that we are dwelling with Him even now.

Likewise, eternal life is not something we will receive when we die; it is something that we receive the moment we put our faith in Jesus—when we are born again. In other words, eternal life is something the believer has right now. Consider a few of the scriptures that communicate this important truth:

- *He who believes in the Son **has** everlasting life* (John 3:36).

- *He who hears My word and believes in Him who sent Me **has** everlasting life, and shall not come into judgment, but **has** passed from death into life* (John 5:24).

- *These things I have written to you who believe in the name of the Son of God, that you may know that you **have** eternal life* (1 John 5:13).

Possessing eternal life now through faith in the Lord Jesus Christ means that we have a vital union with God. We can enjoy this sense of union now, and we will enjoy our union with Him forever.

Part of the blessing of this sense of union is the type of assurance Paul expresses in one of the most powerful chapters in the New Testament—Romans 8. After acknowledging that *"The Spirit Himself bears witness with our spirit that we are children of God"* (Romans 8:16), Paul makes this remarkable statement:

> *So now I live with the confidence that there is nothing in the universe with the power to separate us from God's love. I'm convinced that his love will triumph over death, life's troubles, fallen angels, or dark rulers in the heavens. There is nothing in our present or future circumstances that can weaken his love. There is no power above us or beneath us— no power that could ever be found in the universe that can distance us from God's passionate love, which is lavished upon us through our Lord*

Jesus, the Anointed One! (Romans 8:38-39, TPT).

Another version renders the same two verses,

> *I'm absolutely convinced that noth-ing—nothing living or dead, angelic or demonic, today or tomorrow, high or low, thinkable or unthinkable— absolutely nothing can get between us and God's love because of the way that Jesus our Master has embraced us* (Romans 8:38-39, MSG).

David was persuaded that he was insep-arable from the house of God. We can be persuaded that we are inseparable from the heart of God. He is ours, and we are His.

A Revelation of the
Nature of God

Psalm 23 not only presents the blessings we receive, but there is also a great revealing of God's very nature. His essential character is vividly displayed through David's words. For example, the beginning of this psalm actually presents one of the redemptive names of God: Yahweh-Rohi, meaning "The Lord my Shepherd." *Yahweh* (often transliterated as Jehovah) refers to the self-existing, relational, covenant-keeping God who reveals Himself.

Rohi indicates the tender and compassionate care He provides.

My friend Keith Trump loves the biblical languages and teaches seminars on Hebrew and Greek. Keith shares the following regarding the Hebrew word *rohi* (shepherd):

> People often miss the fact that this particular Hebrew word has another aspect to it. When used metaphorically of God *(The Lord is my shepherd)* it means "God sees those in need and infuses them with empowering grace." Also, *shepherd* remains closely related to the Hebrew word meaning "to see." This reveals the shepherd constantly watching out for our needs. We see this word used very often in the context of the Lord watching over us so we don't

get off course—anything that would take us out of relationship with Him.

It is not surprising that a diamond has many facets, each one revealing the brilliance of the precious stone. Neither should we be shocked that God's nature is revealed through many names, titles, and descriptions in Scripture—each one portraying a different aspect of the magnificence of His person. In the Bible, sometimes an actual name is used, such as Yahweh-Rohi in Psalm 23. In other cases, there is simply a description about God and His works that parallels a name or title given to Him elsewhere in the Bible. Psalm 23 is rich in such descriptions.

With this in mind, we could look at Psalm 23 as follows:

Verse one: He is Yahweh-Rohi (the Lord my Shepherd) and Yahweh-Jireh (the Lord who provides). *"The Lord is my Shepherd, I shall not want."*

Verse two: He is Yahweh-Shalom (the Lord our peace). *"He makes me to lie down in green pastures; He leads me beside the still waters."*

Verse three: He is Yahweh-Rapha (the Lord who heals) and Yahweh-Tsidkenu (the Lord our Righteousness). *"He restores my soul; He leads me in the paths of righteousness for His name's sake."*

Verse four: He is Yahweh-Shammah (the Lord is present) and Yahweh-Nissi (the Lord our banner). *"Yea, though I walk through the valley of the shadow of death, I will fear no evil; for You are with me; Your rod and Your staff, they comfort me."*

Verse five: He is once again Yahweh-Jireh (the Lord who provides), and He is Yahweh-Mekaddesh (the Lord who sanctifies). *"You prepare a table before me in the presence of my enemies; You anoint my head with oil; my cup runs over."*

While Yahweh-Rohi is the only redemptive name of God that actually appears in Psalm 23, it is evident that other descriptions given by David suggest titles of God given elsewhere in Scripture. The ones I listed are just a sampling; it would not be a stretch at all to also see El-Shaddai (the Almighty God) in these same verses. And when David says, *"I will dwell in the house of the Lord forever,"* it is easy to picture El-Olam (the God of Eternity).

As rich as all of these Old Testament terms are in the pictures they paint and the meanings they convey, there is no name

that so beautifully expresses and compre-
hensively captures the essence of David's
Shepherd as does the wonderful name of
Jesus. Peter refers to Him as "the Shepherd
and Guardian" of our souls and proclaims
Him to be "the Great Shepherd" (1 Peter
2:25; 5:4, NLT). In describing Jesus, John
writes that, *"The Lamb on the throne will be
their Shepherd. He will lead them to springs of
life-giving water"* (Revelation 7:17, NLT).

Jesus Himself declares: *"I am the good
shepherd. The good shepherd gives His life for
the sheep. I am the good shepherd; and I know
My sheep, and am known by My own. ...I
lay down My life for the sheep"* (John 10:11,
14-15). When we understand that Jesus laid
His life down for us, we can begin to understand the great love God has for us. David
risked his life for his sheep by fending off a
lion and a bear, but Jesus literally gave His

life for us, dying on the cross to redeem us from sin and death. The implications of Jesus giving Himself for us are enormous.

Paul asks, *"If God is for us, who can be against us? He who did not spare His own Son, but delivered Him up for us all, how shall He not with Him also freely give us all things?"* (Romans 8:31-32). When we describe Jesus as our Shepherd, it is not a mere philosophical thought or theological concept; it is an absolute reality. It is a solid, tangible relationship in that Christ purchased us by His very own blood. The following two statements need to be deeply embedded in our hearts!

For He is our God, and we are the people of His pasture, and the sheep of His hand (Psalm 95:7).

Know that the LORD, He is God; it is He who has made us, and not we ourselves; we are His people and the sheep of His pasture (Psalm 100:3).

Concluding Thoughts

When David first sang, *"the Lord is my shepherd,"* he was giving expression to a profoundly personal faith that came from the core of his being. I pray that you will not simply read Psalm 23 as an outside, objective observer, or simply "parrot" or echo David's words. Rather, I pray that you will truly "own" this psalm. In other words, be fully persuaded of its truths, so they will be just as real to you personally as they were to David on the hills around Bethlehem.

Don't be content with giving intellectual assent to the poetic beauty of this classic piece of ancient literature, but allow these words to be quickened to you in such a way that they flow from the depths of your spirit, just as they did from David's heart more than 3,000 years ago. The Holy Spirit can make Psalm 23 that real to you.

We are privileged beyond measure to have such a wonderful Savior and marvelous Shepherd. As we follow Him and grow in our relationship with Him, we will see tremendous fruit, benefits, and blessings. I pray that you will experience the richness of all that has been described in Psalm 23. May you grow and abound in all that He makes available:

- Provision

- Rest

- Peace

- Restoration

- Guidance

- Security

- Comfort

- Sustenance

- Anointing

- Abundance

- Confidence

- Union

Let me encourage you to read and meditate on the 23rd Psalm using different translations. One rendering I enjoy is provided below, but the nuances and shades of meaning in different versions will bless you richly.

Psalm 23
(The New Living Translation)

The LORD is my shepherd;
I have all that I need.
He lets me rest in green meadows;
he leads me beside peaceful streams.
He renews my strength.
He guides me along right paths,
bringing honor to his name.
Even when I walk
through the darkest valley,
I will not be afraid,
for you are close beside me.
Your rod and your staff
protect and comfort me.
You prepare a feast for me
in the presence of my enemies.
You honor me by anointing my head with oil.
My cup overflows with blessings.

*Surely your goodness and unfailing love will pursue
me all the days of my life,
and I will live in the house of the LORD
forever.*

PRAYER OF SALVATION

God loves you—no matter who you are, no matter what your past. God loves you so much that He gave His one and only begotten Son for you. The Bible tells us that "... *everyone who believes in him will not perish but have eternal life*" (John 3:16, NLT). Jesus laid down His life and rose again so that we could spend eternity with Him and experience His absolute best on earth. If you would like to receive Jesus into your life, say the following prayer out loud and mean it in your heart.

Heavenly Father, I come to you admitting that I am a sinner. Right now, I choose to turn away from sin, and I ask you to cleanse me of all unrighteousness. I believe that Your son, Jesus, died on the cross to take away my sins. I also believe that He rose again from the dead so that I might be forgiven of my sins and made righteous through faith in Him. I call upon the name of Jesus Christ to be the Savior and Lord of my life. Jesus, I choose to follow You and ask that You fill me with the power of the Holy Spirit. I declare that right now I am a child of God. I am free from sin and full of the righteousness of God. I am saved in Jesus' name. Amen.

If you prayed this prayer to receive Jesus Christ as your Savior for the first time, please write to us to receive a free book!

Harrison House Publishers
P.O. Box 310
Shippensburg, PA 17257

About the Author

Bible teacher and author Tony Cooke graduated from RHEMA Bible Training Center in 1980, then studied religion at Butler University and received degrees from North Central University (bachelor's in church ministries) and from Liberty University (master's in theological studies/church history). Tony's passion for teaching the Bible has taken him to forty-seven states and thirty-one nations. Other books by Tony include: *Life After Death*, *In Search of Timothy*, *Grace: the DNA of God*, *Qualified*, *Through the Storms*, *Your Place on God's Dream Team*, *The Work Book*, *Lift*, *Miracles and the Supernatural Throughout Church History*, and *Relationships Matter*. Various titles have been translated and published in nine other languages. Tony and his wife, Lisa, reside in Broken Arrow, Oklahoma, and are the parents of two children.